Welcome to Busy Book 5!

Can you find these things in the book? Write the page number.

The Busy Book helps children develop in the following areas of learning...

 Communication
Learning to speak together in English.

 Leadership
Learning to build relationships.

 Discovery
Building knowledge and awareness of social responsibility.

 Critical thinking
Solving problems and puzzles and learning thinking skills.

 Creativity
Expressing ideas through drawing and making.

 Self-management
Learning to plan ahead to reach goals.

Exploring wildlife

Look, read and write.

beetle   deer   polar bear   tortoise
cheetah   wolf   eagle   camel
kangaroo   crocodile

This animal is half _____
and half _____ .

This animal is half _____
and half _____ .

Now draw and write about your own animal.

This animal is half _____
and half _____ .

Stop the clock!

Can you complete the table in three minutes?

Wildlife...

in hot countries	_____	_____	_____
in a forest	_____	_____	_____
near my home	_____	_____	_____

Wildlife tour

Come on a wildlife tour with me
Look left, look right, we can see...

...a tiny beetle on a rock.
It's colourful and safe.

...a dangerous crocodile.
You'll have to be brave!

...a young, beautiful deer.
It's friendly and it's kind.

...an intelligent eagle.
Look into its eyes!

...an interesting camel.
I think it's very tall.

...a lot of different animals.
Come and see them all!

**Draw a picture.
Write about it.**

Here's a picture of a cheetah.
It's faster than a lion!

Here's a picture of a _____ .
It's _____ than a _____ .

3

That's unbelievable!

1 Giant tortoises can live for longer than 150 years.

2 I'm taller than a camel.

3 I can name five countries that are bigger than the UK.

Wow!

Really?

That's unbelievable!

How amazing!

Write two **true** facts and one **false** fact. Tell your friend. Can they guess which fact is false?

I think number 2 is false!

My Facts. **True** or false?

1: _____

2: _____

3: _____

Now listen to your friend. Write and guess.

1: _____

2: _____

3: _____

Riddle

Who am I?

My 1st letter is in **YELLOW.**   My 2nd letter is in **FOREST.**
My 3rd letter is in **TAIL.**   My 4th letter is in **FUR.**

I am a _ _ _ _ .

Our world

Look and read. Then match the facts to the photos.

Food:

- [a] I usually eat fish.
- [ ] I can survive for a long time without water.
- [ ] I often eat deer.

Shelter:

- [ ] I usually shelter in forest habitats.
- [ ] I live in the desert. It's got a hot climate.
- [ ] I live beside the ocean.

How they live:

- [ ] I live in a group.
- [ ] I live in a pair.
- [ ] I sometimes live and work with humans.

a

b

c

Do it yourself!

Go outside.

What animals can you hear and see?
Draw. Then write about one.

Animal: _____

What do they look like?

_____

What do they eat?

_____

What shelter do they need?

_____

My animal journal

Create your own animal. Write and draw.

Where does it live?

Does your animal have stripes?

Name: _____

Habitat: _____

Climate: _____

Food: _____

Shelter: _____

What does it look like? _____

_____

Is it more intelligent than a wolf? Braver than a lion?

Is climate change dangerous for this animal?

What does it need to survive?

Email a friend about your animal.

Dear _____ ,

This is my new animal! It's a _____ .

It's _____ than

a _____ .

_____

_____

_____

From _____

My favourite activity in this unit:

_____

My favourite fact in this unit:

_____

This unit makes me feel

because _____

_____ .

All about technology

Look at the photos and complete the crossword.

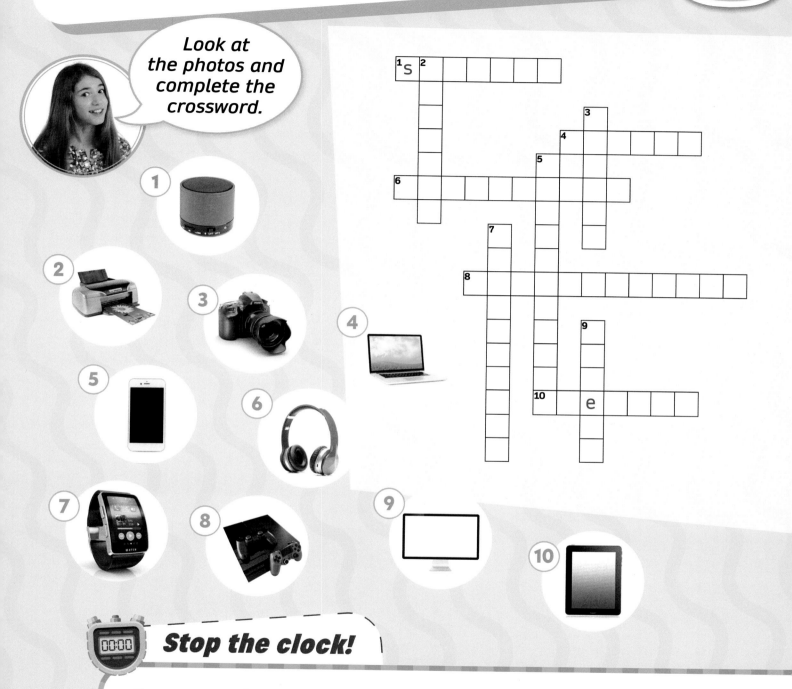

Stop the clock!

Can you complete the table in three minutes?

Technology...

in my home	_____	_____	_____
in a classroom	_____	_____	_____
that I can wear	_____	_____	_____

Imagine with Sam

Class website

Read. Then write about a school activity. Draw.

Hi, I'm Jess. This is our class website. I often upload photos of school activities to our website. My teacher and my friends sometimes write comments. Look, Miss Smith is not happy with Arla's advertisement!

Wall   Find friends   Chat   Profile   Sign out

Olivia is visiting the science exhibition.
Olivia is writing a comment...

Darren is wearing headphones. He often listens to stories in the school library.

Our class maths project.
Ben is writing a comment...

This is my tortoise art project.

Miss Smith: Wow, Arla! I always print photos of my favourite projects. I'm printing a photo of this project for the class display!

Arla: Who wants to buy my bicycle? £50.

Miss Smith: Please don't post advertisements, Arla.

Miss Smith is turning off comments for this post...

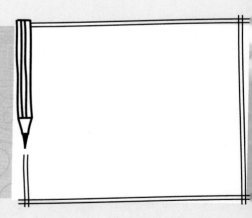

Be safe on the internet: never chat with people you don't know.

Technology advice!

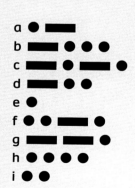

Player 1: Choose one phrase from option 1 and one from option 2 to make sentences. Then tell Player 2.

Option 1

My brother always

My cat often

My sister sometimes

My friend usually

Everyone in my class

_____ never

Option 2

sits on my e-reader.

uses my smart watch.

turns off my speakers.

listens to _____.

posts a lot of _____.

shares their _____ with me.

Player 2: Listen to Player 1. Then choose and write some advice.

You should share your headphones.

You should turn off _____.

You shouldn't post _____.

You _____.

_____

_____

CODE CRACKER

a ● ▬
b ▬ ● ● ●
c ▬ ● ▬ ●
d ▬ ● ●
e ●
f ● ● ▬ ●
g ▬ ▬ ●
h ● ● ● ●
i ● ●

j ● ▬ ▬ ▬
k ▬ ● ▬
l ● ▬ ● ●
m ▬ ▬
n ▬ ●
o ▬ ▬ ▬
p ● ▬ ▬ ●
q ▬ ▬ ● ▬
r ● ▬ ●

s ● ● ●
t ▬
u ● ● ▬
v ● ● ● ▬
w ● ▬ ▬
x ▬ ● ● ▬
y ▬ ● ▬ ▬
z ▬ ▬ ● ●

Morse code is my favourite old technology. What's my favourite new technology?

● ▬ ▬ ● ●	● ▬ ▬	● ▬ ▬ ▬ ●	▬ ▬ ▬	● ▬ ▬ ●

Our world

Read and tick for you.

Quiz

- 🙂 I always write long messages. ☐
- 🤍 I don't like writing! ☐
- 👍 I would like an answer quickly! ☐
- 🤍 I can find a quiet place to communicate. ☐
- 👍 I enjoy reading and writing short messages. ☐
- 🙂 I often send photos to my friends or family. ☐
- 👍 I want to talk to a lot of friends at the same time. ☐
- 🤍 I like seeing people's faces online. ☐

Count and write. You should...

☐ 👍 **chat online** if you enjoy quick communication with friends and family.

• • • • • • • • • • • • • • • •

☐ 🤍 **make video calls** if you don't usually see someone in real life, or if you don't like writing.

• • • • • • • • • • • • • • • •

☐ 🙂 **send emails** if you enjoy writing long messages or sending a lot of photos.

Who do you communicate with often? _____
Why? _____

Do it yourself!

Keep an internet diary. What do you search for online?

Sunday	_____
Monday	_____
Tuesday	_____
Wednesday	_____
Thursday	_____
Friday	_____
Saturday	_____

I often search the internet for _____
_____.

I never search the internet for _____
_____.

My technology journal

Design your own technology. First, think and write.

I often use _____ .

I think young people should _____

but they shouldn't _____ .

I would like to create _____

_____ .

Then write and draw.

It's a _____ .

I'm using it to _____

_____

_____ .

Now post an advertisement!

My favourite activity in this unit:

_____

My favourite fact in this unit:

_____

This unit makes me feel

because _____

_____ .

Order the words. Then use the letters in the red boxes to complete the sentence about Ben.

ezagmina   m ⬜⬜⬜⬜⬜⬜⬜

zupzel   ⬜⬜⬜⬜⬜⬜

yek   ⬜⬜⬜

yomen   ⬜⬜⬜⬜⬜

raidy   ⬜⬜⬜⬜⬜

nagadeb   b ⬜⬜⬜⬜⬜⬜

cansk   ⬜⬜⬜⬜⬜

meleth   h ⬜⬜⬜⬜⬜

What a dark cave!

Ben has to use a ⬜⬜r⬜⬜ and a ⬜o⬜⬜.

Stop the clock!

Can you complete the table in three minutes?

Things I use...

for fun	_____	_____	_____
for every day life	_____	_____	_____
for outdoor activities	_____	_____	_____

Imagine with Sam

Funny email

Complete the emails. Choose or think of your own words.

Add some funny items!

😊 a sleeping bag	😊 blankets
😄 a toy duck	😄 a potato	😊 puzzles
😊 gloves	😊 ropes	😄 a polar bear
😊 a stove	😊 a helmet	😊 a games console
😄 a kangaroo	😊 money	😄 a funny hat

Hi Greg,

Our camping trip is tomorrow!

The weather is colder in the countryside than it is here, so you have to bring
_____ . Don't forget to wear _____ and _____ .

We can use _____ to make dinner and we can play with _____ in the evening.

It's more fun than _____ .

We're going to use _____ and _____ to explore the caves next to the camp.

You have to come to our house at eight o'clock in the morning. Bring _____ .

See you then!

From Tim

Hi Tim,

How exciting! I've got my
_____ . Do I have to bring my
_____ ?
_____
_____

From Greg

Draw the camping trip.

Guess and tick

Play with a friend.
First, read and write.

do your homework

put on a bandage

find your gloves

clean the stove

do a puzzle

make a snack

turn on the _____

use your mobile phone

put on your cycling helmet

make a hot drink

clean the _____

build a sledge

_____

_____

_____

1 Choose five activities. Write each activity down. Don't let your friend see!

1 _____ ☐

2 _____ ☐

3 _____ ☐

4 _____ ☐

5 _____ ☐

2 Guess your friend's activities. Take turns to ask and answer.

Shall I help you clean the car?

No, thank you!

Yes, please! Thank you, that's very kind.

Tongue twister

Can you say this quickly five times?

Clever crabs can colour with crayons and clean crocodiles can climb!

3 Tick the activity when your friend says yes.

The first person to guess all five wins!

Look, read and write.

float   sink   air   flat

Step 1

First, we have to put the hot air balloon on the ground. The balloon uses hot _____ so it can float.

Step 2

Now we can _____ in the sky!

Step 4

When the hot air balloon is _____, we have to pack it away.

Step 3

We have to let the hot air out to make the balloon _____.

Would you like to float in a hot air balloon? Why / Why not?

_____

Do it yourself!

Make a boat that floats.

Use clean rubbish and recycling to make your boat. What things make a good boat? Fill a bowl with water. Does your boat float?

I can use _____

_____

_____

_____

_____.

15

My skills journal

I can run and swim, but I want to learn to climb. I have to practise.

This is me, today.

I want to learn _____
_____ .

I have to _____
_____ .

I need to use _____
_____ .

This is me in _____ years.

Now I can _____
_____ .

I can use _____
_____ .

I feel _____
because _____
_____ .

My favourite activity in this unit:
_____

My favourite fact in this unit:
_____

This unit makes me feel 🙁 😐 🙂

because _____
_____ .

Do you have to have lessons, practise every week or use any special things to learn your skill?

Let's celebrate

Read. Then write and complete the table for Luca, Ben and Eva using the coloured words.

Luca was at the parade. He wore a coat because it was a cold day.

There were balloons at Eva's party. The band was great!

There were fireworks at Ben's festival, and the lights were bright!

There were costumes at the festival.

There was a flag display at the parade, and there were a lot of candles.

There were masks at the party.

	Luca	Ben	Eva
celebration			
clothes	coat		
exciting things			band
colourful things			

 Stop the clock!

Can you complete the table in two minutes?

I celebrate with...

clothes	_____	_____	_____
music	_____	_____	_____
special things	_____	_____	_____

Imagine with Sam

Ask Alyssa

Read the blog. Then write and draw.

Hi! I'm Alyssa.
Welcome to my blog! This is my family. Every year we celebrate the Mid-Autumn festival in China. Usually, there are huge celebrations in our city. This year, there was a parade in the city streets and there were brilliant fireworks. We all had fun!

WolfBoy62 | #1   Reply | Like
When was the parade? What was it like?

AskAlyssa | #2   Reply | Like
It was in the evening. It was colourful and exciting.

Superhero10 | #3   Reply | Like
Who was at the parade with you?

AskAlyssa | #4   Reply | Like
My family and all my friends were there.

BeeBee | #5   Reply | Like
Where were the fireworks?

AskAlyssa | #6   Reply | Like
The fireworks were in the city streets.

FireworkGirl3000 | #7   Reply | Like
Were you tired?

AskAlyssa | #8   Reply | Like
Yes, we were all tired. It was a long day!

_____ | #9   Reply | Like
Were you _____?

AskAlyssa | #10   Reply | Like
_____

_____ | #11   Reply | Like
_____?

AskAlyssa | #12   Reply | Like
_____

Spelling bees

Play with a friend.

Jar:
1 Choose a word from the unit.
2 Ask your friend to spell it.
3 Take turns to ask and spell.
4 For each correct spelling, draw a part of the bee.

The first person to finish their bee wins!

How do you spell parade?

Sorry, can you say that again?

Yes, of course. How do you spell parade?

P – A – R – A – D – E.

Yes! Draw the bee's body.

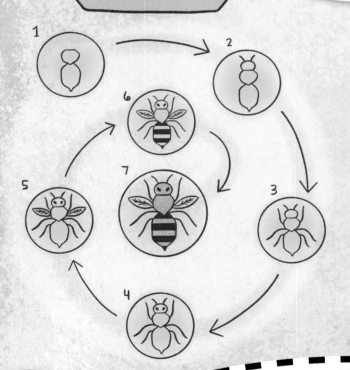

Riddle

What am I?

My 1st letter is in MEAL.   **My 2nd letter is in BEARD.**
My 3rd letter is in EARS.   **My 4th letter is in SPEAK.**
I am a _ _ _ _ _ _.

Our world

Do you know the answers? Go online or ask a friend to find out.

1. What's the first big city to welcome the New Year?

   ☐ Cape Town

   ☐ Auckland

   ☐ Sydney

2. What city celebrates the New Year in Times Square?

   ☐ London

   ☐ New York

   ☐ Tokyo

3. What city celebrates 'Hogmanay'?

   ☐ Paris

   ☐ Dublin

   ☐ Edinburgh

What does Hogmanay mean?

It's the last day of the year, 31 December. It's a word from Scotland.

Do it yourself!

Look up. What can you see in the morning and at night? Draw and write.

We can see a lot of things in the sky, like fireworks, the sun, moon or stars.

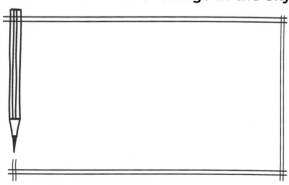

I can see_____ in the morning.

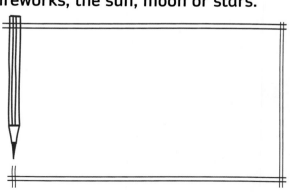

I can see_____ at night.

My festival journal

Choose or imagine a special festival. Draw and colour.

What was the festival's name? What does it mean?

Where was the festival and when was it?

Was there a parade or any special food? Were there costumes?

Hi, _____,

This festival was called

_____.

_____

_____

_____

From _____

My favourite activity in this unit:

_____

My favourite fact in this unit:

_____

This unit makes me feel 😣 😐 😊

because _____

_____.

Can you talk about your festival for two minutes?

Play with a friend. Say the sentence when you land on a photo.

I tidied up the rubbish yesterday.

You need:

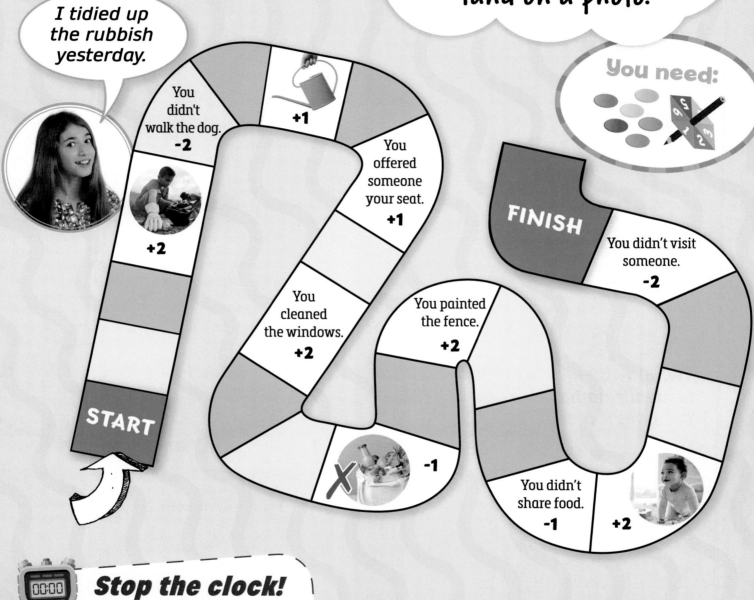

Stop the clock!

Can you complete the table in two minutes?

I can...

share			
tidy up			
paint			

Where are the... ?

Think. Write two foods you can bake.
Then choose four character names.

Food 1: _____

Food 2: _____

Now, put your chosen food
and names in the play.

Boy 1: _____

Boy 2: _____

Girl 1: _____

Girl 2: _____

In the living room.

[Girl 1] _____ : Hi, _____ **[Boy 1]**. When did you arrive?

[Boy 1] _____ : I arrived at five o'clock.

[Girl 1] _____ : What did you bake?

[Boy 1] _____ : I baked some _____ **[Food 1]** and
a lot of _____ **[Food 2]** to share.

In the kitchen.

[Girl 1] _____ : Where did you put them?

[Boy 1] _____ : They're on the table... Oh no – they're not there!

_____ **[Boy 1]** *is trying not to cry.* _____ **[Girl 2]** *and*
_____ **[Boy 2]** *arrive.* _____ **[Girl 2]** *opens the cupboard.*

[Girl 2] _____ : Your party food is safe. I'm looking after my little brother,
_____ **[Boy 2]**. He's very hungry!

_____ **[Boy 2]** *points to the food, now on the table.*

[Boy 2] _____ : Shall I help you to eat the _____ **[Food 1]** and the
_____ **[Food 2]** now?

_____ **[Girl 1]**, _____ **[Boy 1]** *and* _____ **[Girl 2]**
laugh and smile.

[Boy 1] _____ : Yes, you can!

Act out
the play with
friends!

23

The big interview

I'm going to interview

- ☐ my friend
- ☐ my brother
- ☐ my sister
- ☐ _____

Smile, you're on television!

Hi, _____ ! What did you do today?

_____

Did you smile today?   **Yes / No**

Why did / didn't you smile?

_____

Did you laugh today?   **Yes / No**

Why did / didn't you laugh?

_____

Did you _____ today?   **Yes / No**

Why did / didn't you _____ ?

_____

CODE CRACKER

My favourite band posted a new song on the internet and I liked it. What's it called?

Our world

What did you do to help your family, school or neighbours this month?

- [ ] I walked a dog.
- [ ] I tidied up the rubbish.
- [ ] I donated my old toys or clothes.
- [ ] I carried shopping for _____.
- [ ] I looked after my _____.
- [ ] _____
- [ ] _____
- [ ] _____

Let's volunteer!

What skills can you offer a community project?

cleaning

painting

visiting people

collecting money

I am good at
_____.

Do it yourself!

**Find out about a project in your community.
What did they do this year?**

The project is called _____.

This project is [ ] cool [ ] brilliant [ ] amazing.

This year, they _____ because _____

_____.

My kindness journal

Read and think. Then add your own ideas.

My 10-day Kindness plan

Day 1
Tidy up the rubbish.

Day 2
_____
_____
_____

Day 3
_____
_____
_____

Day 4
_____
_____
_____

Day 5
Make food for my family.

Day 6
_____
_____
_____

Day 7
_____
_____
_____

Day 8
_____
_____
_____

Day 9
_____
_____
_____

Day 10
_____
_____
_____

Choose your favourite kindness day. Draw and write.

How did you feel?

When I helped, I was _____ because _____.

My favourite activity in this unit:

_____

My favourite fact in this unit:

_____

This unit makes me feel

because _____

_____.

26

Our important places

Read. Complete the crossword.

Across

2 travel by b _____ _____

5 go on a t _____ _____ _____

6 take a t _____ _____ _____

8 read a g _____ _____ _____ _____ book

9 wait in a q _____ _____ _____

10 stay in a h _____ _____ _____ _____

Down

1 pack a
s _____ _____ _____ _____ _____ _____

3 Exchange m _____ _____ _____

4 go s _____ _____ _____ _____ seeing

7 buy a t _____ _____ _____ _____

 Stop the clock!

Can you complete the table in two minutes?

Things I need...

to pack			
to buy			
to do			

27

Holiday plans

Draw and label Dasha's travel journey.

Hi Dan,

I'm excited... I'm going to go snowboarding next week! I'm going to visit some famous mountains - the Alps!

First, I'm going to take a taxi to the airport because my city doesn't have an underground. Then I'm going to fly over towns, countryside and rivers to the Alps.

Then I'm going to travel by coach or minibus to a small village. I'm going to put my suitcase in the hotel and then I'm going to take a cable car to the top of a mountain and go snowboarding all day!

From Dasha

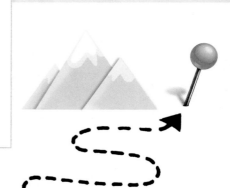

Choose one and tick. Then read and write.

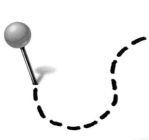

1 When are you going to go?
2 Where are you going to stay?
3 How are you going to travel there?
4 What are you going to do?

1 _____

2 _____

3 _____

4 _____
_____

Do you agree?

Read and Complete.

Group 1

flying in a hot air balloon

swimming with _____ (ocean animals)

going sightseeing by _____ (a way to travel)

buying a ticket to see _____ (a band or singer)

sleeping in a tent in _____ (a place)

Group 2

more exciting

scarier

cooler

more boring

more fun

better

Group 3

watching fireworks at New Year

waiting in a queue to meet _____ (a famous person)

staying in a big hotel in _____ (a city)

watching a / an _____ (an animal) parade

going to a / an _____ (a food) museum

*Swimming with sharks **is more** exciting **than** watching a penguin parade. Do you agree?*

Choose one from each group. Write sentences.

Now find people who say...

	Yes, I agree!	No, I disagree!
1 _____	_____	_____
2 _____	_____	_____

Tongue twister

Can you say this quickly five times?

Spike's telling Stella a space story.
Steph's telling Spencer a spy story.

Our world

You're the magazine writer! Finish the text.

Accommodation

If you're going to stay in a tent, you must tidy up. Plastic rubbish stays on Earth for 500 years! You should _____ _____.

This hotel is cold: between –3°C and 5°C. A good sleeping bag is very important! You should also bring _____ _____.

Culture

A bus tour is a good way to go sightseeing. You can learn a lot of interesting information about a city.

_____
_____

Some festivals are older than you might think. The Venice Carnival started in 1162!

_____
_____

Souvenirs

Upcycled bags are good for the environment.

_____
_____

Local food and drink make good souvenirs. There are many different cheeses to choose from in Spain!

_____
_____

Do it yourself!

Find out. Then draw.
What eco-friendly souvenirs can tourists buy in your country?

_____
_____
_____

My travel plans journal

Stick in photos, draw and write.

Things to think about:
- How am I going to travel?
- Where am I going to stay?
- What places or festivals am I going to visit?
- What wildlife am I going to see?
- What skills am I going to learn or use?

_____
_____
_____
_____
_____

One day I'm going to travel to

_____.

My favourite activity in this unit:

_____

My favourite fact in this unit:

_____

This unit makes me feel

because _____

_____.

Goodbye

About me

My favourite activities in this book were...

_____

_____

Interesting facts I learnt...

_____

_____

I'm going to celebrate finishing the book by...

_____

_____

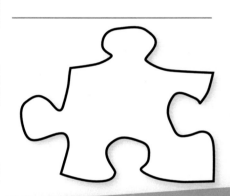

Rise and Shine Certificate

You finished Busy Book 5!

Well done!

Awarded to: _____

Age: _____   Date: _____

Nadia
Nadia

Bella
Bella

Sam
Sam

Leo
Leo

Alex
Alex